Secret Genealogy VII

DNA… Jumping into the Gene Pool. A High-Tech Gathering of the Tribes

Suellen Ocean

Secret Genealogy VII
DNA… Jumping into the Gene Pool. A High-Tech Gathering of the Tribes

by

Suellen Ocean

Published by:
Ocean-Hose
P.O. Box 115, Grass Valley, CA 95945
www.oceanhose.com

Also by Suellen Ocean:

Secret Genealogy
Secret Genealogy II
Secret Genealogy III
Secret Genealogy IV
Secret Genealogy V
Secret Genealogy VI
The Lies of the Lion
The Guild
The Last Quadroon
The Celtic Prince
Black Pansy
Blue Violet
Black Lilac
Ellie
Rose Thorn
Mississippi Wild Blue
Scarlet Lobelia
Gold River
Gone North
Chimney Fire
Hot Snow
Acorns and Eat'em
Poor Jonny's Cookbook

Table of Contents

Introduction

As I sit down to write this book, it feels like Biblical end times. Today any way. The forest outside my Northern California house is so dry and leafless, it looks like a fire swept through, only it hasn't. Not yet anyway. But it has swept through much of California and news reports are that the flames move the distance of a football field, every three seconds. Yesterday, there were sirens, helicopters and spotter planes. Today it's quiet. Social media relays to me that *many* people in the small country town where I used to live, have lost their homes. The flames were too quick for humans to save anything but their lives.

And there are rumors of war. We don't need war. We need acceptance and togetherness that brings peace for our children and grand-children. That includes us. *We are* the grandchildren. We are those who came later. We are the children of those Biblical stories. We are the children of the survivors of war. We are the children of those who were persecuted by fire, whether it was the Inquisition or the Calvary upon the villages of the Natives who were here long before Europeans. We are here because someone was here before us. You're reading this, because like me, you want to know as much as you can about them.

There are various ways that we can uncover our origins. We can ask relatives, search genealogy sites, conduct library research and lately… have our DNA tested. When we take a DNA test, we produce a batch of data that can be used for future research. Our information is added to the data base of DNA understanding.

Yesterday, I received the results of my "spit test" from 23andMe. I thought that you might like to come along as I explore what it means. It's a whole new realm so, there are a lot of questions. Thanks for joining me on this quest. I hope this research will help you learn more about what *your* DNA says about *you*.

One
I Thought I Was… But the Test Doesn't Show It

To be honest, it's hard to understand DNA science but I know that with everything, there's a learning curve. So… the more I delve into it, the more I'll understand. But because it's complex, I'm going to keep this topic as simple as I can. Rocket scientists can bow out now.

DNA testing companies are not guessing at your ancestry but their system is not perfected. The science is still in its infancy and progress relies on millions **more** people signing on, so that there will be more genomes to compare. And for all I know, the company could be spewing nonsense at me and I wouldn't know the difference. I forked out a hundred dollars. I may have paid to be a guinea pig.

If you've read my other books, you know that I've researched my ancestors. So looking at my DNA reports did not bring **immediate** surprises. But I was surprised by what *wasn't* there. I mean, come on. Three of my *Secret Genealogy* books are about finding hidden Jewish ancestry. The DNA testing company couldn't have left that out. But they did. They list Ashkenazic Jews but they said nothing about Sephardic Jews which is what I believe some of my ancestors were. I wrote to 23andMe with this question:
What about Sephardic DNA? I see no mention of it.

They answered with:
There are no definitive ways to tell for certain if you have Sephardic Jewish ancestry based on your DNA. For this reason, we do not identify Sephardic ancestry in our reports.

They refer me to their guide so that I can "read about the population selection process."

Where is Sephardic ancestry hiding and why? What a pity that it's hidden. Secret genealogy is still secret. It never ends. Even in the days of lab testing our saliva. Maybe it's hidden in the "unassigned category." That expression made my sister cringe. Why? Does she think we're aliens? Here's what 23andMe has to say about the unassigned category:

There is a wide range of human diversity out there and sometimes our algorithm is unable to assign a region of DNA to a specific population. As we collect more data and update our algorithm, we expect that the amount of unassigned ancestry seen by customers will decrease.

Or maybe my Sephardic Jewish ancestry is hidden in the "Broadly Southern European" category. I think we need to make a call out, to our Sephardic friends to have their DNA tested, so that those of us with *unassigned ancestry* can be *assigned.* That said, these DNA tests mean different things to different people. We need to respect that. My son's fiancé related strongly to her Italian heritage. She was very disappointed that the percentage was smaller than she expected.

And then there's the "Broadly European" category. "Sometimes a piece of DNA matches a regional population but cannot be assigned to a more specific population. In such a case we assign the DNA 'broadly' to that regional population rather than a specific one." That's fancy speak for *we don't know.* And that's okay. I'm happy with what they've given me. It's better than nothing.

So, my conclusion here is this. Don't be dismayed if your DNA test doesn't confirm your research, that tells you that you have Sephardic Jewish ancestry. I think that the testing company that I used, 23andMe, just doesn't have enough Sephardic Jewish DNA samples. It's completely understandable that people would have apprehensions about giving up DNA for a data bank. Giving up your DNA sounds absurd really, when you think about it. But there are those of us who are so obsessed with genealogy that we give a piece of ourselves (and our privacy) just to know. Or to verify. That said, there are scores and scores of Ashkenazi Jews sharing their DNA findings. (See chapter eleven *Eureka! Finding the Gems Hidden in DNA Reports* for an independent Sephardic GEDmatch/Genesis search.)

My daughter-in-law ordered DNA tests for herself and my son. When they got an earful around the campfire one night, they changed their minds. I thought about listening to the horrible things that *could* happen but decided against it. There are both good and bad things that come with science. I think that getting my DNA tested was a good thing. It verified my research and as I studied it further, I eventually found a few surprises.

Quote
"…it's the minority ancestry many testers are seeking. That which we cannot see in the mirror and may be obscured in written records as well, if any records existed at all."
Genealogist Roberta Estes

Two
DNA, Chromosomes, Haploids… Enough Already

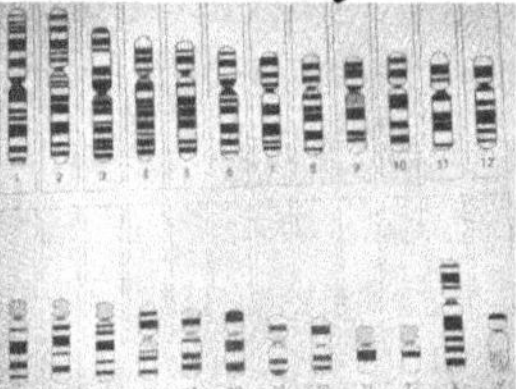

This is the way scientists illustrate our twenty-two
chromosomes, plus the X and Y.

In our cells, we have forty-six chromosomes. They
are divided into pairs, making twenty-three pair.
Forming the pair are: one copy inherited from our
father and one copy inherited from our mother.
Starting with chromosome one, the top left
chromosome on the chart, we see that it is the largest.
The chart shows the chromosomes decreasing in
size, until you get to the twenty-first chromosome, it
is the smallest. That little chromosome, number
twenty-one, is the smallest human chromosome and
only represents one-and-a-half to two-percent of the
total DNA in our cells. The one next to it, is the
second-smallest, that is chromosome number
twenty-two. The last two chromosomes on the chart
above are the X and the Y chromosome.

Each person normally has one pair of sex
chromosomes in each cell. The Y chromosome is
present in males, who have one X and one Y
chromosome which makes their "one pair," while
females have two X chromosomes that make their
"one pair."

You will receive several reports from the DNA
testing company. One of them is a *haplogroup
report*.

haplotype – human mitochondrial DNA sharing a common ancestor.

haplogroup - A group of humans with similar haplotypes who share common maternal ancestors.

Your DNA is "typed" and then it is "grouped." We may never completely understand the science but that doesn't stop us from grasping a good portion of our DNA reports and what they tell us. Through the haplogroup reports, I can trace my ancestry from my mother through her mother, going back through the ages. Men can do the same through their father's haplogroup. Half of a woman's DNA comes from her father but we don't inherit Y chromosomes, so women don't have paternal haplogroups. To discover your paternal haplogroup, you'll need your brother or your father to take the test. Together, you get a closer look at your paternal ancestry. If having a brother or father take a test is not an option, you can ask a male cousin to share his paternal haplogroup report. The DNA testing company might not connect that report to yours, like they would for a father or brother because the lab doesn't do that yet. You'll have to study it on your own and see if you can find connections. A male first cousin who was your father's biological nephew, will have the same haplogroup as your father or brother.

DNA (*deoxyribo nucleic acid*) is a nucleic acid found chiefly in cell nuclei, important in the transference of genetic characteristics and in synthesizing protein.

In college, in 1989, I took a biology class called "Plants and Civilization." The professor, Dr. Quibbel, discussed DNA and warned us that in our lifetime, we might see some unusual creatures. He was referring to gene manipulation. The mapping of the genome was not completed until fourteen-years later, in 2003, but he saw the implications. If agriculturalists create tomatoes that have genes from chickens, what's next?

I remember Dr. Quibbel saying that plants are more like their grandparents than their parents. I think he said people are like that too. So, I dug out my class notes and rummaged through them. I did not find anything about dog-humans, nor that about being more like our grandparents. But I did find some elementary notes:

DNA is self-replicating, holds our content. This molecule likes to "bring the biosphere in." DNA "wants to conquer the universe."
DNA is a very stable molecule. Amazingly accurate – provides info on how an organism lives and replicates.
Humans are Diploids. We reproduce by producing HAPLOID GAMETES (one).

Plants and animals with rare exceptions are:
Diploid (2n) - 2 sets of chromosomes
* from male parent
* from female parent
Each kind of chromosome is present twice
Homosapiens – 23 pairs (46 chromosomes)
Kinds: 23 from father… 23 from mother

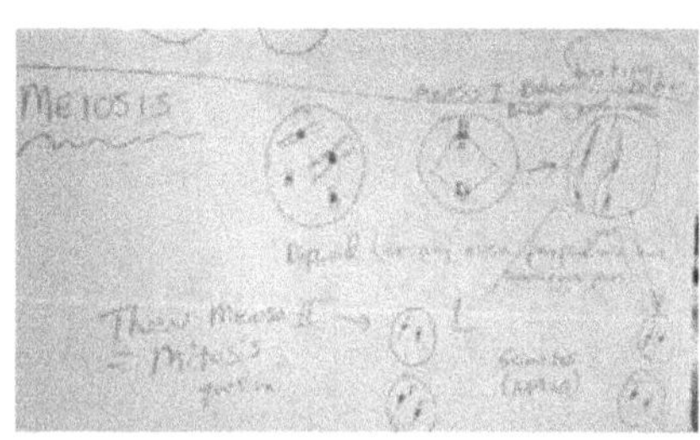

Here are some pictures that I drew from Dr. Q's drawings on the chalk board. I add them here as a prelude to the chromosome charts you'll see when you get your DNA test reports back. If you're intimidated and want to give up, think of these little drawings. A little biology helps.

Chromosomes – separate packages of DNA (library for growth development)

23andMe has what they call **The Chromosome Painting**. They describe it as "an in-depth way of looking at your Ancestry Composition results. It shows a colorful representation of the 23 sets of chromosomes that make up your genome."

Geneticists use a locus to position a gene on a chromosome. Locus comes from the Latin word for "place." Or, another way to put it, "locality." In a given chromosome, we can characterize where the gene resides on the chromosome, on a particular locus. This is another drawing from my biology notes. The black dot on the locus is a chromosome. The chromosome chart is just a way of showing where the chromosomes reside. Where they are located, tells us a lot about our biological traits.

Haplogroups

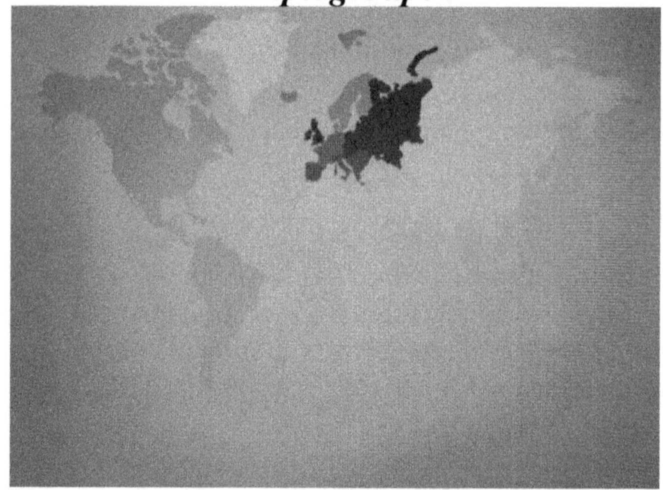

The shaded parts on the map are the areas where my modern ancestry resided.

At first, I wasn't impressed by my haplogroup reports. There were maps and arrows pointing the migration patterns of my haplogroup. It looked generic. Not specific to me but to millions of people. But it was what I was given (and paid for) so after the disappointment wore off, I returned to the colorful maps and pictures and wondered if I couldn't glean something that made me feel special and not just another descendant of a primitive human traipsing through history.

My haplogroup report tells me that I "descend from a long line of women that can be traced back to eastern Africa over 150,000 years ago." If that's the case, why do my other reports show my ancestors as mostly European? Where are my Eastern African ancestors?

mtDNA - mitochondrial DNA, inherited solely
from the mother

Here's the thing. Today's DNA testing is done on **two** sources. It's done on the DNA found in our twenty-two pair of chromosomes and in the little bit of DNA found in our mitochondria. Most of our DNA is bundled in our chromosomes but our mitochondria also have a little bit of DNA.

Mitochondria DNA is labeled mtDNA. To help me remember, I see the *mt* and think… mother. Because it is the mtDNA that comes from my X chromosome that I received from my mother. There is an uninterrupted line from every woman to her mother, her mother's mother, etc. We descend from that female line. Men also receive mtDNA from their mother. That is where the DNA comes from that the testing company uses to find your haplogroup. But as far as the uninterrupted line, for men, it descends from their father and the DNA comes from the Y chromosome that they inherit from their father.

mtDNA:

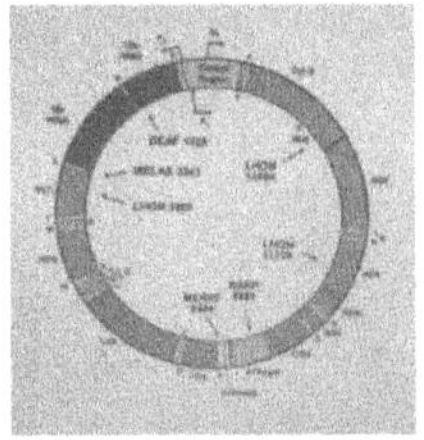

"Mitochondrial DNA is typically diagrammed as a circular structure with genes and regulatory regions labeled."
Source: National Institutes of Health, Genetics Home Reference.

Quote
"Your Ancestry Composition report shows the percentage of your DNA that comes from each of 31 different ancestry populations worldwide. We calculate your Ancestry Composition by comparing your genome to the genomes of over 10,000 people with known ancestry. When a segment of your DNA matches the DNA from one of the 31 populations with high probability, we assign that ancestry to that

segment of your DNA. We calculate the ancestry for individual segments of your genome separately, and then we add them together to get your overall Ancestry Composition."
https://www.23andme.com/ancestry-composition-guide/

Three
Sharing and Finding Relatives

If you already know your genealogy, DNA testing can validate your findings. It doesn't prove it but sort of. It's as good as it gets. For now. But it might be like telling you, who your father or mother is. *You already know that.* Unless of course, you haven't been told the truth. The DNA testing company warned me that there might be surprises and that I might discover something unpleasant. If you don't know who your biological parents are, it could be a great way to find them, provided they or their close relatives have also taken the test. I'm sure there are both positive and negative outcomes and no doubt sometimes feelings get hurt. This should be considered before undertaking the test and publicly revealing your results.

If you don't have a clue what part of the globe your ancestors inhabited, DNA testing will at least give you that. But the problem is, it's rather current. What about our ancient ancestry? It's as if our ancestors left a shadow where they *were.* The longer they've been gone from their corner of the globe, the fainter their shadow. Oral history and text can't always be proven. That's okay. When science catches up with the truth, there will be vindication. It might be four-hundred-years from now but who's counting?

A cousin found me on ancestry.com and we both like to talk. A lot. What I mean is, we have obviously inherited a "friendly" gene. We email back and forth. He did his DNA test through ancestry. I did mine through 23andMe. We want to compare our results, so he told me about https://www.gedmatch.com. At GEDmatch, you'll use what's called your "raw data." Because I got my test from 23andMe, they had a spot on the GEDmatch website for me to upload the raw data. I had to download it first from 23andMe but it was easy. Then I uploaded it to GEDmatch.

Quote
"GEDmatch is a FREE, non-profit, "do-it-yourself" genomics website that allows DNA testers to upload raw data from FTDNA, AncestryDNA, and 23andMe to compare with a large database of data that has been voluntarily uploaded by other testers. A description of the types of comparisons will follow. GEDmatch uses a slightly different algorithm for the comparison so some additional matches may be available, as well as some different views of the comparisons. This can also help provide contact information for some matches. Everyone should take advantage of this opportunity. GEDmatch is not affiliated with any of the testing companies. The http://www.GEDmatch.Com site provides tools for making 'deep' comparisons between genealogies and DNA test results to help identify possible hidden ancestral connections with distant cousins. This is particularly useful when your GEDCOM or list of DNA matches contains hundreds, or even thousands of individuals. This service is provided free to anybody."

I did not find GEDmatch easy to understand but I intend to figure the site out so that I can utilize it. But I must admit, the more that I delve into the new science of DNA, the more I appreciate good old-fashioned genealogical sleuthing. I am fortunate that so many of my family lines have preserved records that have been shared for years. But for those whose ancestors are unknown, especially in cases of adoption, there are a lot of unanswered questions. With today's DNA science, adoptees can find answers. And if genealogists use both, DNA testing

and old-fashioned research, the two fit together well. You may find it very gratifying to have your research verified. The DNA reports are like the answer sheet to a quiz. How many questions did I get right? Some of the things that we come up with during our research, seem outlandish but when the DNA reports come back to us, the truth fits, just like Cinderella's slipper.

Within all populations, there are people who are friendly and their lives are an "open book," while others are cautious. At 23andMe, there's a box where you can send a message to your "predicted" cousins. My initial thoughts were, "Hey this is fun." But I'm glad I contacted very few of the "relatives" that are listed. GEDmatch has a little warning about etiquette. It is considered spam to fire off a lot of emails to people without investigating first.

Since I'm reporting my findings as they happen, truth be told, I'm finding that beyond the initial reports that 23andMe sent me, which were fairly easy to understand, the process of finding ancestral clues through strangers on GEDmatch, who all have long lines of numbers attached to their emails, is like trying to solve a difficult math problem. The "it's not rocket science" jokes might not apply here. What I don't like about these websites full of numbers and links is the same thing that I don't like about many genealogical websites. *Information Overload.*

That said, I'm impressed with the intelligence of my fellow genealogists. It requires not only patience but focus. As for the "fun" I was hoping to have, finding cousins through DNA, my hopes, at first, were dashed. If you're an adoptee expecting to find biological parents and siblings, these things take time. I suspect that many people upload their raw data and don't know what to do next.

Being that I don't usually like to ask people for help (I feel like a pest) I wasn't sure that I would spend much time chasing after 3rd, 4th and 5th cousins on GEDmatch who could care less that I came along. Why should they? There are eight-hundred people that arrived before I did. They may be sick of it. "You're a third cousin? And the big deal is?" But little by little, "cousins" have been sending requests, wanting to share reports.

For instance, 23andMe tells me that they can determine whether I share identical segments of DNA on one or both copies of each chromosome. They claim that I share 0.20% of my DNA with a man named Stephen. "Stephen is your 4th Cousin (predicted)." And then it shows my 22 chromosomes plus my X and shows a spot on the 7th chromosome. They have colored it purple and say that it's "half identical." How that little piece of my 7th chromosome tells us that we are 4th cousins, well… that's beyond me. But they "predict" that it's true. I'm guilty of overthinking it but I can't move on unless I accept the charts and the science.

I thought that I could look at the chromosome chart and study it and that would tell me how I am related to Stephen but apparently not. I have to share my surnames and he has to display his. That is the only way, other than, "Well, my great-great-grandmother was from Ireland," that sort of thing. If you think that DNA testing is the end all, it's not. It is a brand-new beginning to a whole new realm of genealogy. Receiving answers, connecting to others, filling out your profile. There is a lot of work to do. That said, cousins pop up like dandelions after sunshine and a spring rain. We are related to a lot of people. Figuring out how you connect, that's the grunt work.

Four
Am I my Brother's Keeper?

I sent a text message to my brother Michael: *If I pay for it, will you take the DNA test? It is the only way that I can see my paternal DNA. A father or a brother.*
His reply: *No needles?*
Me again: *No. You spit in a tube and I'll mail it in.*
Michael: *Ok!*

I was quite surprised by my brother's response. I was prepared to enlist my sister's services and gang up on him. He's a very private person. He "hates" Facebook and never wants anyone to know any of his business so I consider it a big responsibility to protect his privacy. But DNA testing for genealogical research and finding cousins is **not** private. We give up a lot. Sort of makes you think of the saying, *What do you want? Blood?* No, your spit will do.

You just never know how family members will respond. I almost didn't ask my brother to participate because I was pretty sure he wouldn't be interested. Once his kit arrived, he came running over. This is the guy who got mad at me because I included his name on the front of an envelope I sent to my mother's house. He doesn't want anybody to know anything about him. He's not a criminal, he's a professional security guard and has to pass criminal background checks. He was a soldier for years in the National Guard. He's a good chap. But he's very private and obstinate about protecting his privacy. But he came running over. I think it made him feel important. And he felt good about helping me discover my paternal genetic history. And he was probably *curious*. Isn't that why we do it?

Watch out for curiosity. They're not kidding when they warn you that you might discover things that you don't want to know. Especially if you take the test and receive the reports for both health and genealogy. What could happen? You could find out that you're in danger of inheriting a fatal disease. That would mean that your children could inherit it too. Taking the test won't change that either way but some people don't want to know. I don't think I would. You may have low odds of inheriting something but that would not stop your imagination. That said, there are plenty of people who are testing their DNA for their health reports. With excellent reasons for doing so. It makes sense. One must think these things through, before stepping into that world.

And what responsibility do others have if it turns out there's a brother out there that you didn't know about? A sibling that you had no idea existed? You test your DNA solely for the purpose of genealogy and then all hell breaks loose. As my brother said when he left the house after submitting to the test, "Someone could contact me and say, I'm your son!" We got a good laugh out of that. He's never been married and I would not call him a playboy. But you just never know. If I was on the other end of that, and was adopted and didn't know who my biological parents were, geez Louise, I'd be submitting my DNA to every one of the testing companies. Because thousands of people are joining, it raises the odds of finding "family." Whether they will be welcoming or not depends on a variety of circumstances. Let me tell you a little story.

I have a friend who was adopted as a baby. She had a wonderful life. The couple who adopted her were wealthy and they loved her as their own. But of course, my friend wanted to know who her biological parents were. Let's call my friend "Mary." Mary took a DNA test and immediately matched up with a woman who was so closely related, she could have only been her biological mother or aunt. The woman turned out to be her aunt whose only reason for testing her DNA was to explore her ancestry. She had *no idea* that her sister had given birth to a baby girl and given her up for adoption. In fact, the aunt was so sure of this, Mary had a hard time convincing her to ask her sister about it.

Mary's biological mother, let's call her Peg, hadn't told a soul about her fling with a handsome pilot nor of giving birth to a child. She was slender and had hidden it well, was very young, went out of town for a while, had the baby and gave her up for adoption. Peg kept it all a big secret. Peg went on to have a successful marriage and three children. Still keeping it a secret.

I have not pried into Mary's situation. Last I heard, the aunt was working on a meeting between Peg and her biological daughter Mary. Even though you know you don't have a biological child looking for *you*, your brother, sister, cousin or parent could. And then one is forced into a predicament. Be prepared for surprises.

About ten years ago, I helped a friend "Mindy" find her biological half-brother. Mindy's father died. He had fathered a child when he was a teenager and the baby was given up for adoption. He had wanted to find his child but died before finding him, so Mindy wanted to find him and I wanted to help. There are people on the Internet who spend their days helping unite biological families. In a month or two, we found Mindy's half-brother, thanks to these kind people.

The other day, I ran into a friend. When I told him that I was writing about DNA testing, he got excited and told me his adventures with two companies. I knew that he was adopted at birth, so we immediately cut to the chase. He found his biological family and he is thrilled about it. "After fifty-eight years, I finally know who I am," he told me.

DNA testing is addictive for some folks. The testing companies are well aware of the hunger we have for it. They encourage us to have our parents, grandparents, aunts, uncles, cousins and especially brothers and sisters take the test. The reason is because we don't inherit everything from our parents. So, whatever we didn't inherit, a relative may have. And there can be drastic differences. I could have next to no Eastern European results while my sister could have more than thirty-percent. That's why people enlist their relatives. It's an obsession.

Five
A Few Words on Blood Types

I have an unusual blood type, Rh-negative, that gave me a clue to my ancestry. I knew that the odds were high that my ancestors were either Basque, Moroccan Berbers, ancient Iranian Jews or Oriental Jews of Israel. When I received my DNA reports and saw the maps that showed the trail of my ancestors, it came as no surprise. Blood… what does it tell us?

We inherit our blood type from our parents. Dennis O'Neil, of the Anthropology Behavioral Sciences Department at Palomar College in San Marcos, California, has mapped out the distribution of blood types worldwide (see bibliography). Professor O'Neil believes that it's a "false assumption that humans can be unambiguously placed into 'races' on the basis of selected traits such as skin color, hair form, and body shape." He believes that racial classification "has more to do with cultural and historical distinctions than it does with biology." We should all keep that in mind when we chose to have our DNA tested. What is it that we're seeking? Are we looking for our "race?" With the knowledge that there are no distinctive races, only one race, the human race, we still seek answers to who our ancestors were. What color was their skin? Were their eyes round or slanted. Were they tall or tiny? Who were these people that if we were closer to on the ancestral line, we may have bonded with and possibly loved in the way that we love our parents?

One of the reasons why DNA testing can be disappointing is if we are looking for racial classifications that professor O'Neil warns against. People are dark skinned because their ancestors were from hot, sunny climates. People are white skinned because their ancestors came from cold, sun-less climates. As children, we're taught about the different peoples of the world and I think we want simple answers like that. But we will never get them. In the words of professor O'Neil, "The more we study the precise details of human variation, the more we understand how complex are the patterns. They cannot be easily summarized or understood."

To see the blood type distribution maps, go to: https://www2.palomar.edu/anthro/vary/vary_3.htm

Combined with professor O'Neil's information and a little research that I did on my own, here's a little more information about blood types:

Blood type A – It can be found in Montana in the Blackfoot Indian population and it's also found among the Australian Aborigines. It reaches even higher levels in Northern Scandinavia. According to Stanford university, 35.7 % of the world has A positive and 6.3% has A negative.

Blood type B – It is highest in Central Asia with high "pockets" in Africa. Type B is also common in Eastern Europe. According to Stanford university, 8.5% of the world has B positive and 1.5% has B negative blood type.

Blood type AB – The rarest blood type. Blood type AB has both A and B antigens. According to Stanford university, 3.4% of the world has AB positive and 0.6% has AB negative blood type.

Blood type O – Within the indigenous population of Central and South America, blood type O is almost 100%. Other populations with high rates of blood type O are Australian Aborigines. It is found in high numbers in Western Europe, particularly in those whose ancestors were "Celtic." According to Stanford university, 37.4% of the world has O positive and 6.6% has O negative blood type.

<u>Rh Blood type</u> – Blood types A, B, AB and O, can be Rh positive or Rh negative. (The plus or minus sign next to your blood type signifies whether you are Rh positive or Rh negative. Most of the world's population has Rh positive blood type. The Basque population has the lowest rate of Rh positive and even they come in at 65%. Other populations high in Rh negative are the Oriental Jews of Israel, ancient Iranian Jews and Moroccan Berbers. If your blood type is positive, it contains the Rhesus D antigen. If it is negative, it lacks the Rhesus D antigen.

Quote
"D antigen is a protein with many parts, found on the surface of red blood cells. The D antigen is also known as the 'Rh factor,' and it tells your blood type. People are either D (Rh) negative or D (Rh) positive. If your blood type is D negative, your red blood cells do not have the D antigen."
https://www.sharecare.com/health/blood-basics/what-is-d-antigen-rh-factor-blood

Six
Expecting Too Much from Your DNA Reports

Manolis Dermitzakis, a genetics professor at the University of Geneva is quoted in a 2015 businessinsider.com article about race and ethnicity. (See bibliography.) Dermitzakis argues that ethnicity and race are man-made ideas that have no basis in genetics. The article reminds us that the only thing DNA shows us, is that we're related to a large group of people who live (or lived) in a certain geographical region. I read the article just days after I received my DNA results. I appreciate the reminder because I came away with that same thinking. The author of the article, Kevin Loria writes:

Quote
To tell people their ancestry, consumer DNA testing companies compare markers in customers' genes to markers from other people around the world that are in their databases. They use those markers to give you as close an approximation to your "ancestry" as they can.

Loria quotes Dermitzakis as being, "… a bit worried about these companies." He wonders whether we are interested in "current populations or ancient." That is what disappointed me too. I know who my recent ancestors were. I want to know who and where *their* ancestors came from. You risk disappointment if you expect too much from your DNA reports.

When my mother visited San Francisco in about 2007, she could not get over the population change. San Francisco has always been populated with people from around the globe but according to my mother, the demographics have changed dramatically. The Bay Area has a magnetism (and Silicon Valley) that draws people from many countries. A genetic sample of the population that was there in the 1950s would be different from one taken today. And we must never forget that Native Americans lived in the Bay Area for thousands of years. And before the Mexican American War, Mexican ranchos dotted the California countryside. They still do, of course, but today two Bay Area cities, San Jose and Oakland, hold two of the ten spots on the list of "most diverse" populations in America.

Let's use Holland as an example. Even the native Hollanders aren't native all the way through their heritage. Some like to claim that their ancestors have been there for hundreds of years. Some would say a thousand years. But even someone whose ancestor was there a thousand-years-ago, was probably from Southern Europe first and migrated or was driven to the cold north. Sephardic Jews were driven to the Netherlands during the Inquisition. That was over five-hundred-years ago. Their descendants are still there. Yet, our ancestry reports are not going to inform us that our ancestors were Sephardic Jews, they are going to report them as Northern European. There's nothing wrong with that title but it gives us very little history and makes me appreciate the research that we, as genealogists, do.

As the DNA testing companies collect samples to load into their database and compare them with ours, we get more truth. And that is that humans are migratory creatures. That said, these companies have an allure. I tested myself and then wanted my husband to try it. And then my brother… well, you get the point. Genealogy is a family saga. We want to know what happens next. DNA testing is just another tool and I suspect that it will improve over time. Especially when there are more samples and more history accompanying it.

And then there's the issue of how *small* the DNA is that we've inherited from our ancestors. And the issue of it not showing up at all because it is so small. This is where I get emotional but I can't help myself. I *feel* the ancients who came before me and contributed to my being. Our domesticated dogs came from primitive wolves. The ancient DNA is diluted but you can see the connection when you look at your dog's teeth. If we overlook those ancestors whose DNA **does not** appear in our reports, we're missing something very important. We are a composite of those who came before us. Whether their DNA has "washed out" or not. Hopefully, advancements in genetics will reveal more. Even though it's not revealed, the essence of our ancestors is there. Let's not lose sight of that.

When I got my reports back and said to my husband, "I'm two-percent Native American," he answered, "Is that all?" Let me tell you, that took the wind out of my sails and I had just jumped in the boat. I was so proud of that two-percent. I guess it depends on how you look at it. Science can throw you off that way. There are people who say that our bodies are 65% oxygen, 18% carbon, 10% hydrogen, 3% nitrogen and 4% other. We *know* that we're *way* more than that. We're fathers, mothers, brothers, sisters, gardeners, swimmers, soldiers, politicians, mathematicians, GENEALOGISTS, etc. We mustn't let the fact that our genetic inheritances are small, or non-existent, discourage us. Our ancestors are counting on us to tell *their* story. Because their story is *our* story, whether their DNA shows up on our reports or not.

As of the writing of this book, there are not enough "reference populations" for the DNA testing companies to use as comparison. Here's what I think's going on. Let's say that you got a job at a laundry mat. The owner set six laundry baskets in front of you. You are to sort all the socks that come through the laundry mat. By color. Red, green, blue, yellow, white and black. The newer the sock, the more color it has. That's easy, you throw all the new black socks into the black basket. Same thing with the white socks. Easy, toss it in. But the white socks that have been around awhile, might have traces of green grass stains or red food coloring or someone threw the whites in with the darks so they're no longer completely white. What should you do? If someone threw a red blouse into the white load of laundry and the socks turned pink, should you still throw them into the white basket or should they now go into the red basket? Imagine if you were asking a computer to make that decision. And you probably thought right away, only six baskets? There are as many colors of socks as there are color crayons.

What happens when the owner of the laundry mat comes back and expects to see six baskets of socks, all appropriately organized by color. You had to make the call, so the light pink socks went into the white basket. The dark pink socks went into the red basket. Beige socks into white, brown socks into the black basket. I used color as an analogy but we could use teeth. Think of all the different types of teeth humans have. We could never put them into six categories, there must be thousands of teeth types. *Genealogy is fluid. People are diverse.*

People who test at multiple companies say they get different results. Some companies are better at picking up small percentages. Some companies draw their maps differently. We should not be surprised that they are having a hard time categorizing us by our DNA. It was never meant to be that simple. But if you want absolute answers to your genealogy, DNA sampling is only a tool. The companies will tell you that.

So where's the magic? That elated feeling you got when you found out that your great-great-great-grandmother was from a foreign land. And your DNA shows no trace of it? What do we do then? How do we explain away that feeling? That connection? That pride of knowing who we are? We don't explain it away. We build on it. It was not washed away. It was absorbed. In a different way. One that you can't touch or put under a microscope and explain with numbers. No, I'm not a science denier but I'm not an ancestor denier either. There's got to be more to the story. And some day, science will laugh at these early DNA tests and how people ran to them by the thousands to find out who they *really* are. Who are we *really*? We are the embodiment of those who came before us. Whether the computer spews out a place marker for them or not, our ancestors cannot be denied. It runs much deeper. Those of us whose ancestors look over our shoulder and guide us, *we know*. Discussing it with my husband, he has this to say. "We may have inherited Native American instincts for spirituality but they don't have a marker for that yet." What else have we inherited that there are no markers for?

In her blog (dna-explained.com) Roberta Estes, states that the latest technology "…is not really ripe yet for that level of confidence except perhaps at the continent level and for people with Jewish heritage… So assigning a specific 'ethnicity' to you is a matter of finding the best fit – in other words which population you match at the highest frequency for the combined segments being measured." Makes me think of pink socks. She states that "…one company groups the Czech Republic and Poland in with Western Europe and another groups them primarily with Eastern Europe but partly in Western Europe and a third puts Poland in Eastern Europe and doesn't say where they group The Czech Republic." Estes further states that "… you're not necessarily comparing apples to apples."

I'm glad that she pointed that out. There are cultural, religious and political differences between Eastern and Western Europe. That's not insignificant, especially if you're trying to uncover Jewish ancestry. One does have to pay attention to the colored maps that are provided with your DNA reports but heed the warnings.

Seven
Using a Forensic Lab to Retrieve a Deceased relative's DNA

I have a relative who works for a criminal attorney, so I asked her, "Where can I get a family DNA sample analyzed? My father is deceased but I still have his shaving brush. It must have his DNA on it. I'd like to test it for ancestry." She said to, "call your local sheriff's office forensic crime lab." I thought that was a great idea but I sat on the idea for over a year. Finally, today, I put a call in and was referred to the "property unit" where I reached an answering machine. I have no idea if they will return my call. In the meantime, I contacted 23andMe and asked them:

My father is deceased but I have kept his shaving brush. Can I get his DNA off of that? Do you know how I can test it?
Thanks, Suellen

Hello Suellen,
Thank you for your interest in 23andMe. The analysis that we provide can only be performed using a saliva sample collected using the saliva kit that we include with your order. The saliva sample collected is ~2 ml. Unfortunately, we are unable to analyze any other type of sample. Additionally, our service is designed for individuals to have full control over their genetic analysis and the resulting data. Accepting a customer's saliva sample for processing implies that the person providing the sample has read and agreed to our Terms of Service, our Privacy Statement and our Consent Document. It implies that the person is a willing participant with access to a computer to view their results. In short, our service cannot be used by deceased persons both logistically and from a legal perspective. I am not able to

So even if I was successful in obtaining my father's DNA from his shaving brush, 23andMe only accepts saliva samples and only from the living. Katy is right. I need to do an internet search. Time for some sleuthing. What shall I google? *Retrieving DNA from a dead person's comb to trace their ancestry?* Actually, yes, that works well. It led me to Arc Point Labs. Their web page tells me that "Most states do not have laws relating to collecting DNA from deceased persons, and so individual estate representatives are largely free to decide." Okay, sounds good, so far.

"Attorneys are beginning to advise their funeral home clients to counsel family members that at the time of a loved one's death is the last best chance to secure such direct samples." Something to think about but my beloved father died in 1990. Reading further, they advise, "If direct DNA samples of a deceased person are not collected, 'touch DNA' may be collected from their personal belongings, but it is more expensive and less certainty that reliable results can be obtained." The only thing that bothers me is the "more expensive" part. There's expensive and there's *expensive*. This next part is encouraging, "…the increasing sensitivity of DNA testing allows more reliable results with smaller and smaller samples. A new subset of the DNA science called 'touch DNA' can identify separate individuals from fewer than ten distinct skins cells collected from

items handled casually by different people —
samples that are invisible to the naked eye." Surely,
they can find some DNA on my father's shaving
brush. They have a hundred nationwide locations in
America and a spot to type in your zip code. I found
an office in the city closest to me. I clicked on
Solutions for Individuals and then **Testing for
DNA**.

"Need to solve a question of paternity for legal
reasons? Searching for more details on your
ancestors or information on your ethnicity?
Deoxyribonucleic Acid testing, better known as
DNA testing, unlocks answers and reveals
information hiding within our cellular structure. If
you have questions about your paternity, maternity,
or distant lineage, turn to DNA testing — the most
accurate and available technology to determine
biological relationships — at ARCpoint Labs."

They do say "ancestors" and "ethnicity." There is a
spot to contact them so I will. If only to find out just
how *expensive* is expensive. Scrolling down further,
past the "contact us" button leads me to six different
categories and buttons, including, **Ancestry Testing**.
*"When you want to learn more about your family's
genetic background, including regions ancestors
lived, our ancestry DNA testing provides answers."*
I'll bet 23andMe gets this question all the time and
they know that ARCpoint Labs provides this service.
The big question is how much is it going to set me
back? Here's the note I sent them:
*I would like to know what it costs to perform "Touch
DNA" on my deceased father's shaving brush. And
also, what the process is. Thank you.*

Shortly thereafter, the phone rang. It was ARCpoint.
The man on the phone told me that, "DNA ancestry

tests just tell you that you're a human being. We are a lab. We don't deal with uncertainty." He also used the expression "no concrete results" and told me that my 1990 sample was too old. When I asked about cost (just curious) the total for paternity, by comparison, was about $450. But for some reason, he changed his tune and told me to try Heritage.com and that maybe my sample wasn't too old after all and that he was sure Heritage is much cheaper.

Heritage.com takes me to a money management site so it's back to Google and "who does touch dna for ancestry?" That brings up all the usual DNA testing companies but also dna-testing-advisor.com. Their web pages have some great tips like DNA is only found in the roots of hair so cut hair won't work. And this one. It's discouraging:
"If you touch an object with the subject's DNA on it, you can contaminate it with your own DNA, rendering it useless. Also, samples should generally be stored in dry paper envelopes rather than plastic bags."
And this: *"Keep in mind that any lab will charge you for ATTEMPTING to extract DNA. You pay the fee whether they find any useful DNA or not."* Sounds… expensive. And like other sites, there's the discussion about exhuming dead bodies. Now that really sounds expensive. And creepy. I'm not that obsessive about genealogy. We all have our limits and that's mine. My father and his good sense of humor would laugh about that for days. Seriously, I am about ready to give up. But they have recommended Roberta Estes blog post on forensic DNA testing. I've already discovered Roberta and quoted her more than once. Let's give her the last word.

Her blog post, "Digging Up Dad, Exhumation and Forensic Testing Alternatives," is highly entertaining but I have abandoned my fantasy of extracting DNA from my father's shaving brush. I doubt that I would find any success and I would spend a fortune trying. I will add Roberta Este's blog post to the **Interesting Websites** chapter and as promised, give her the last word. "There is new technology on the horizon that will only need one cell of DNA."

Preparing Ahead for Your DNA Test

Once you get your DNA kit and you're ready to spit into the tube, the instructions ask that you don't eat or drink for thirty minutes before hand. One of my cousins coerced his stubborn brother to take the test so that he could have more family DNA to study. He had already taken his own test through Ancestry.com so thought he may as well test his brother with another company. He mentioned that he was concerned about his brother's denture glue interfering with the test. Sure enough, he has been contacted by the company and told that the spit test needs to be taken again. So, let me start by saying, go over the directions carefully and see what they advise. It might save you the trouble of redoing it. Someone else told me that the DNA sample that they sent, never did come out right and that the company gave up on them after several tries and they were not offered their money back. I heard this from one of my distant cousins participating in a group email. I thought it was worth noting.

Once I decided I was going to get my DNA tested, I was so anxious, I just went for it. Now that I've received my reports, I'm having to backtrack and do a little homework because honestly, I don't understand what the DNA report is stating, in a number of areas. It may as well be ancient Egyptian, it's that foreign. But like all things, the more you hang out with it and let it sink in and return to your reports, again and again, it starts to make sense.

If you have a lot of time to kill and you love genealogy, you'll love filling out all the information fields the DNA testing company offers. But I haven't even finished filling out my family tree on ancestry.com. I had no idea that 23andMe would want me to provide family tree stuff. I should have assumed but I was so excited, I did not think of it. Those who take the test through ancestry.com can tie their DNA reports into their already existing family tree and merge with others whose DNA matches. Something to think about.

The truth is, all the different DNA testing companies have something to offer. And their results can be different too. If you decide to go with more than one, you won't be the first. I've run across many people who test widely.

Eight
Getting Involved with Someone Else's DNA reports

I'd be willing to bet that the majority of those reading this will sooner or later get involved with someone else's DNA reports. Because we have so many familial connections and because genealogists are passionate about their research, one test leads to another and another and another. If it wasn't so expensive, I'd do more. If they were free, I'd have everybody over at my house spitting in tubes. I just hope that this new research is used for the better good. I'd hate to have it come back and haunt us.

My "other" reports are my brother's and my husband's. I have complete control over those reports because they gave me permission. As a genealogist, you understand how exciting this is. I spent decades looking for my husband Jon's ancestry. It wasn't easy. Can I tell you another story?

Jon had a grandmother with a fantastic tale she told about her family history. It almost sounded made up. She claimed that she descended from the same regal line as Winston Churchill. Winston was a "cousin," she told everyone. And because she was so proud of that, she used the Churchill name. She went by Bonnie Churchill. Try googling Bonnie Churchill. Good luck finding *anything*. Bonnie Churchill is a famous columnist whose prolific prose is everywhere. I mean *everywhere*. Talk about hogging up the world-wide web. Not her fault of course but I could never get to the bottom of Jon's ancestry with that obstacle. That and the fact that Churchill is very common and like Bonnie, people were not afraid to use that surname even if they had another one. But try, I did. Again and again. I went to libraries too, bringing home books on Winston Churchill because Bonnie had claimed that she descended from Sarah Churchill and Bonnie always insisted that she was a first cousin to Winston. Knowing what I know now about Churchill genealogy and DNA, I'd bet the farm that Bonnie was not first cousin to Winston.

But Bonnie loved to tell the colorful story of her proud illustrious history. The story was that Sarah Churchill fell in love with a French Canadian Indian (by Indian I mean native). His surname was Taylor and he played the violin like a master. His fondness for alcohol also made it into the story so it must have been obsessive. The story goes that when Sarah ran off with him, the illustrious English Churchills disowned her.

Sarah was Bonnie's mother. When Sarah was hospitalized, Bonnie was adopted by another family. During the 1930's, when Bonnie became an adult, she started an all-girls band. Bonnie was the band leader. Jon remembers seeing pictures of can-can girls that were in his grandmother's band. The story continues with intrigue when Bonnie's band travels to Berlin and Hitler's soldiers arrest her and throw her in jail, supposedly for having two Jewish girls in the band. Bonnie tells everyone that her friend, Mae West bailed her out of jail.

So now Bonnie is on her way home, back to America. On the ship, she meets a wealthy younger man and they fall in love. They marry on the ship. Their marriage does not survive but their togetherness has brought the birth of a baby girl, my husband Jon's mother. Unfortunately, Jon's mother did not live long enough to verify these anecdotes. She passed away when Jon was only ten.

Bonnie Churchill's story sounds almost too outlandish to be true. It was twenty-five years before I found anything on this ancestry, much less confirming these stories. Finally, I came across an obituary that had Bonnie's brother's name, Robert Taylor. The statistics matched with the few tidbits that I had. That obituary opened a whole new world of ancestry. Bonnie was indeed a Churchill and indeed had Indian blood and indeed has a pedigree of aristocratic French and English ancestry. She was not lying about her romance on the ship back from Berlin or stretching the truth about the wealthy young man she married. His father was a developer in Shaker Heights, Cleveland, Ohio. He built a subdivision of little houses that imitated Shaker Heights mansions. Having achieved success with his tract of bungalows, he lived in one of the mansions. Not to downplay the significance of building a neighborhood of fabulous little homes, they're delightful. But they are not mansions. They are *imitating* the mansions. Bonnie's stories are true in spirit but they may be bungalows instead of mansions. I think she's guilty of elaborating them up a bit. Maybe it was the wine talking. I have to hand it to her though, she wasn't lying. If she saw the huge file that I've collected of her ancestry, she'd be proud. And to tell you the truth, the French Canadians in the original story sounded poor and rag tag. Their ancestral files tell me otherwise. Somewhere along the way, Bonnie's family, met hard times. Stories were told to her and she repeated them. But judging by the genealogical record that I've uncovered, Bonnie Churchill's ancestry was not shabby.

It's fun to find royalty in our family lines. And it's nice to know that we had ancestors who were prominent and successful but far too many people are looking for illustrious ancestry to fulfill something lacking within ourselves. I'm just as proud, if not more so, of my salt-of-the-earth type ancestry as I am of those who have historical status. Just sayin'.

I have set up my account to have all the DNA reports that I manage, come to me. 23andMe lets you do that easily. The other companies are probably similar. I'm surprised at how easy it is to take someone else's DNA and manage it. Shouldn't it be protected, like a social security number? Maybe it will be, later in the game. Right now, it's a brave new world and they're giving us free reign.

My husband's reports came from the same testing company but they're different than mine. He received his maternal *and* paternal haplogroup because he has inherited the X and Y chromosomes. I only received my maternal because women do not inherit Y chromosomes. And my first reaction to his reports is the same incomplete feeling that I had with mine. Eventually, the anticlimactic feeling goes away and appreciation sets it, but only if you study them.

Because I am managing my husband's and brother's accounts, I am receiving requests from other participants to view their reports. I set it up so that people had to request to see them. I also have a cousin who jumps in with information and names and questions. It's a lot of fun and as the days pass, my understanding of human beings and our connection to the past, grows deeper. As does my respect for life.

Nine
Eureka! Finding the Gems Hidden in DNA Reports

Before we talk about finding the gems hidden in your DNA reports, we need to discuss how they're found. Their found in "snips," a catchy word for *single nucleotide polymorphisms*. SNPs.

Genetic scientists pursue snips that identify certain **populations** that can be tagged to geographical locations. (The word populations is used instead of ethnicities.) But snips are not exclusive to one group. They can be shared by all peoples. Geneticist John Hawks, "How African Are You?" writes that, "It's now possible to test quickly for hundreds of SNPs by using special microchips that bind to the distinctive DNA sequences. These tests examine hundreds of SNPs at once; if among these a person has many that are common in Africa, it is likely that she has some African ancestors." This is done by performing (with the computer) **genetic admixture tests**. The tests look at the DNA that we've inherited.

Geneticist Hawks writes about Greeks and Ashkenazi Jews who may have Native American affinity. "So, maybe this 'Native American affinity' reflects the scattering of alleles by prehistoric Asian nomads to the ancestors of Greeks and Jews as well as to American Indians." DNA testing is being studied by some Native American communities, whose oral history tells them that they have a connection to the Israelites. But Hawks writes, "As far as anthropologists know, there were no lost tribes connecting Greeks, Jews, and ancient Americans." That's a discussion that has been going on for probably two or three-hundred years and will continue. Greeks and Ashkenazi Jews can puzzle over their admixture tests that show Native American affinity but what about those who are seeking verification that they have Cherokee or Iroquois ancestry? If they have Greek and/or Ashkenazi Jewish ancestry and Native American genes show up, how do they differentiate?

So the truth is, because humans are intricately connected, sorting them into populations isn't easy and our DNA tests can be misleading. That said, science does have something to offer. So, let's go to the website called GEDmatch.com and have some fun. (Or Genesis, the new search engine/algorithm **on the GEDmatch home page**. They plan on merging the two. Think of Genesis as a room in GEDmatch's house.) 23andMe folks are sent to the Genesis room where you can find various populations and other genealogists with which to compare.

Note… *download* means you send it from their computer to yours. *Upload* means you send it from your computer to theirs.

Before you can enter your DNA results into GEDmatch, you will need to upload your *raw data* to their website. No matter where you took the test, you will first upload it to GEDmatch. They will send it to the Genesis "room." Before you can do that, you have to download it from your DNA testing company. (For 23andMe people, you'll find it in **Tools… Browse Raw Data.** Then look for the download option.) Once they email it to you, save it to your computer and then go back to GEDmatch.com and upload the raw data from your computer to theirs. If your DNA test was taken through companies like MyHeritage, WeGene, FTDNA, Ancestry or another, you will also use the

GEDmatch raw DNA upload utility. After you log-in to GEDmatch, it's found on the right-hand side of the webpage. Look for: **File Uploads - Raw DNA file Uploads** to find the utility.

After you have successfully uploaded your raw data it may take a day or two or three before you can start playing with it. They will give you a *kit number*. This is the number that you use to run your DNA results. If you're a 23andMe person, you must use **Genesis**. Like I said, think of it as a room in GEDmatch's house. After you log in, there's a lot of info on the GEDmatch page. It's not clear where Genesis is. Go to the bottom right of the GEDmatch page. **Genesis Beta.** "Accepts raw DNA data from companies previously not compatible with GEDmatch. New algorithm with lower thresholds and better accuracy. Welcome." Click on: **Find more about Genesis Beta.** That will take you to the Genesis "room."

Now we want to take advantage of Gedmatch's "admixture proportions calculators" which I like to call *look-ups*. Look for **Admixture/Oracle with Population Search.** It will ask you what population you want to search. If you leave it blank and click "Find," it will pull up all populations in all oracles. Find a population you're interested in and enter your kit number. You can only choose one population at a time. If you get an error message, you probably neglected to click on the population. Usually in less than a minute, the results pop up. All the results for the look-ups that I did, had a pie graph listing percentage as well as a list.

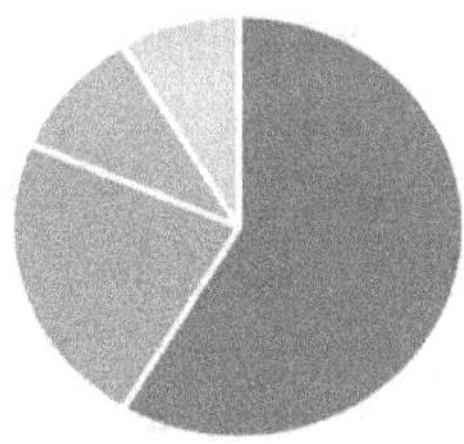

Oracle machine
In complexity theory and computability theory, an **oracle machine** is an abstract machine used to study decision problems. It can be visualized as a Turing machine with a black box, called an **oracle**, which is able to solve certain decision problems in a single operation. The problem can be of any complexity class. Even undecidable problems…
Wikipedia

I'm sure you have to be signed in to run your kit number through the various Genesis oracle fields but if you want to take a peek at the list of populations you can explore, here is the link to the list. https://genesis.gedmatch.com/ap_pops2.php?pop

Initially, I filled the field out with "Jew." I had to scroll to the bottom to enter my kit number. And I could only select one search item at a time. Below, you'll see the results that I received from a calculator listed as "Jew Ashkenazi." The smallest population percentages are often **left out** of the pie-shaped graph they provide but appear in the written chart. Even if you're not Jewish, or Alpine or any of the hundreds of population titles, run you're kit number through different ones and see what happens. Genealogy is supposed to be fun, isn't it? I cannot find the name of the person who developed the calculator for the results below. The only reference I have is an email address. Dilawerkh4@gmail.com. When I did a Google search using this email, I found an informative blog about using GEDmatch. You'll find it in the *Interesting Websites* chapter of this book.

EHG stands for "Eastern European Hunter Gatherers," WHG stands for "Western European Hunter Gatherers," SHG stands for "Scandinavian Hunter Gatherers," CHG stands for "Caucasus Hunter Gatherers," and EEF stands for "European Early Farmers."

<u>"Jew Ashkenazi"</u>

SE_ASIAN	-
ANATOLIA_NEOLITHIC	11.61 Pct
CHG_EEF	47.17 Pct
POLAR	0.67 Pct
EHG	17.42 Pct
SUB_SAHARAN	0.30 Pct
IRAN_NEOLITHIC	-
KARITIANA	0.45 Pct
ANCESTRAL_INDIAN	1.91 Pct
NATUFIAN	3.20 Pct
SIBERIAN	-
PAPUAN	0.29 Pct
SHG_WHG	16.96 Pct

I had a lot of fun de-coding this, it's much different than my DNA reports from 23andMe. I used Wikipedia and looked up the population groups, like KARITIANA. I copied and saved a paragraph about the people and looked at the pictures of the people and saved a few images. These are all in my computer and my genealogy scrapbook has taken a high-tech gathering of the tribes look.

I don't know how accurate these different admixture calculators are. I have extensive genealogical records and I don't know if it's just emotional but when you do a lot of these look-ups and they're similar, you get a sense of what's true. Occasionally, a calculator appears skewed, especially if I choose a population that's an unlikely match. However, many of the calculator's results are similar to the stats that 23andMe gave me but with more detail. The large DNA testing companies are *playing it safe*.

You have to keep scrolling to the bottom with every new search and put your kit number in. Write down which look-up you're on because otherwise you'll get confused. The computer doesn't keep it marked when you return to the list. They're all so interesting, you're going to want to look at all of them but it will take you months of all-nighters. You might want to start at the top, keep track of which one you're on and go down the list. Look-ups that share the same calculator might be similar. You'd have to go through all of them and compare. It's better to go into this with some organization. A pencil and pad next to you is a grand idea. Or even better is to copy and paste the line you're working on and then you can copy the results beneath it.

Each look up has the **project**, which is the name or abbreviation of the project, the **calculator** that is used to decipher your kit number and the *title* of the **population**.

If you want to find Native American, try searching for "North_Amerindian" without the quotes. "Arctic_Amerind" is listed in one of my results but I did not find it as a population to search. But if your native ancestry is from Canada or the Eastern United States and they travelled south over the generations, keep "Arctic_Amerind" in mind. Also search for the tribe. I saw Apache and Navajo. I didn't find Cherokee, that surprised me. If you have roots in the Western United States, especially California, try "Mexican" and see what comes up. "African_American" is another you might try if you're looking for black ancestry. Make sure that you include the *underscore*. "Eskimo" is another one to try if you're searching for Native American ancestry. There are thousands of population groups listed. You might want to go to the list **first** so that you get an idea of what you can look up.

If you leave the search field blank, it will pull up all populations in all oracles. The whole list of possible searches comes up. Let's hope that busy anthropologists took DNA samples from the primitive tribes that they studied and that their research is included in these admixture calculators. The wording on some of the calculators, make it appear to be the case. Here is one example:

Quote
The Near East Neolithic 13 calculator is based on the recently recovered ancient genomes from the Near East. The genomes were described in a recent 2016 paper, "The genetic structure of the world's first farmers," by Losif Lazaridis et al.
http://biorxiv.org/content/early/2016/06/16/059311

It's important for us to have a place in this world. Knowing the migrating paths of our ancestors brings a sense of connectedness. For the ancients, their connection to the past was through oral history. Today, we have "snips" and "admixture calculators." And I hope, more a sense of what unites us. These are not races, just population groups in a constant state of flux. After you run your kit number through various look-ups, you get a strong sense of your population groups. There's variation between the look-ups but there are consistent population groups that come up so frequently, you'll memorize them.

Merging your DNA reports with good old-fashioned genealogy

Let's say that your 23andMe DNA report lists this:
Southeast Asian < 0.1%
"You most likely had a fourth great-grandparent, fifth great-grandparent, sixth great-grandparent, or seventh great (or greater) grandparent who was 100% Southeast Asian. This person was likely born between 1670 and 1760."

Look up the definition of Southeast Asia. It's a geographical subdivision of Asia that includes the following nations: Burma, Cambodia, Indonesia, Laos, Malaysia, the Philippines, Singapore, Thailand, and Vietnam.

What does this bring to mind? Does your old-fashioned family history record your Dutch ancestors as working for the East India Company in the 1600s? The Dutch were in Indonesia during the 1600s. That might be where the Southeast Asian ancestry comes from.

Or… maybe you had an ancestor who jumped ship. Today, it's called St. Bernard Parish in New Orleans but a small fishing village called Saint Malo used to stand there, before a hurricane destroyed it. It was America's first Filipino village, founded by deserters who jumped from Spanish ships around 1763.

DNA findings can enrich our family histories. Hopefully, they bring answers and more questions because if there are no questions, what fun is that for future genealogists? Our work has just begun.

Interesting Websites

https://www.youtube.com/watch?v=acGJmLlsWg4
&feature=youtu.be

http://eternidad-
haplogrouph.blogspot.com/2011/09/origin-
haplogroup-h-is-descendant-of.html
This blogspot has a beautiful Celtic soundtrack that
plays while you read it. *Go for the music.*

http://www.y-str.org/p/ancient-dna.html
Fun to look and see if you match up with ancient
DNA taken from world-wide publicly available
samples.

Reddit has an interactive map, Largest Y-DNA
Haplogroup by Country, World Map:
https://www.google.com/amp/s/amp.reddit.com/r/da
taisbeautiful/comments/6jstfk/largest_ydna_haplogr
oup_by_country_world_map/

An interesting distribution map of mitochondrial
haplogroups in Europe, the Middle East and North
Africa:
https://www.eupedia.com/europe/maps_mtdna_hapl
ogroups.shtml

http://www.telegraph.co.uk/news/science/science-
news/10486479/Phobias-may-be-memories-passed-
down-in-genes-from-ancestors.html

Mitochondrial DNA Results - What Do They Mean
and What Do I Do With Them?
by Roberta Estes,
http://www.dnaexplain.com/Publications/PDFs/Mt
DNAResults.pdf

A humorous and informative Roberta Estes blog post:
https://dna-explained.com/2013/04/30/digging-up-dad-exhumation-and-forensic-testing-alternatives/

An in-depth look at GEDmatch admixture calculators:
http://genealogical-musings.blogspot.com/2017/04/finally-gedmatch-admixture-guide.html

Your DNA kit begins a 'journey of discovery' – but are results in safe hands? by Tim Johnson, The Sacramento Bee, December 4, 2017
http://www.sacbee.com/news/business/technology/article187617963.html#ampshare=http://www.sacbee.com/news/business/technology/article187617963.html

Bibliography

Plants and Civilization, taught by Dr. Charles Quibell, professor of botany, Sonoma State University, 1989.

http://www.businessinsider.com/what-genetic-testing-can-tell-you-about-race-or-ancestry-2015-11, Race and ethnicity have no real biological meaning, by Kevin Loria, Nov. 20, 2015.

https://dna-explained.com/2016/02/10/ethnicity-testing-a-conundrum/
2/10/2016 by Roberta Estes

https://blogs.ancestry.com/ancestry/2014/03/05/understanding-patterns-of-inheirtance-where-did-my-dna-come-from-and-why-it-matters/

Understanding Genetics, by Dr. Aaron Shafer,
Stanford University, 3/17/2006.
http://genetics.thetech.org/ask/ask166

National Institutes of Health: US National Library of Medicine:
https://ghr.nlm.nih.gov/primer/genomicresearch/snp

Why Do We Inherit Mitochondrial DNA Only From Our Mothers? by Steph Yin, June 23, 2016.
https://www.nytimes.com/2016/06/24/science/mitochondrial-dna-mothers.html

Mitochondrial DNA and Ancestry - Tufts University,
http://ase.tufts.edu/chemistry/hhmi/documents/Protocols/Maternal%20Ancestry_Introduction_Reworked_Aug_25_2011.pdf

Medical Daily, The Grapevine, "Why Is AB Blood Type So Rare? It's All About The Red Blood Cells," by Susan Scutti, Mar 25, 2016. Newsweek Media Group.
http://www.medicaldaily.com/ab-blood-type-red-blood-cells-379342

"Distribution of Blood Types," by Dennis O'Neil, Professor Emeritus, Anthropology Behavioral Sciences Department, Palomar College, San Marcos, California.
https://www2.palomar.edu/anthro/vary/vary_3.htm

https://www.sharecare.com/health/blood-basics/what-is-d-antigen-rh-factor-blood

"How African Are You? What genealogical testing can't tell you," by John Hawks.
http://www.slate.com/articles/health_and_science/science/2006/03/how_african_are_you.html

Story about the earliest Filipinos to Louisiana:
https://en.wikipedia.org/wiki/Saint_Malo,_Louisiana

23andMe: DNA Genetic Testing & Analysis
https://www.23andme.com/

ARCpoint Labs:
https://arcpointlabs.com/individuals/dna/forensic-dna-evidence/deceased-dna-matching/

DNA Testing Adviser.com, The Independent Guide to DNA Testing, Forensic DNA Testing
for Paternity & Genealogy: http://www.dna-testing-adviser.com/Forensic-DNA-Testing.html

www.ingramcontent.com/pod-product-compliance
Lightning Source LLC
Chambersburg PA
CBHW050701250726
48662CB00002B/787